KiDS'
PARTY FOOD

KÖNEMANN

Planning a party

When it's time for your child's birthday party, a little forward planning will help to make the very special day a great success. Whether the party is to be a simple morning play time for toddlers, a full scale, dress-up extravaganza for six-year-old children or a sleep-over for pre-teens, work out the relevant details beforehand with the guest-of-honor.

A few weeks before the date, decide where your party will be held, what kind of party, how long it will last and how many guests to invite. Your child should make the guest list; even young children have definite ideas on who they want to ask and what type of party they would like to have. If you can't cope with a large number, say so at the beginning and give your child a number to work with; for example, six or ten guests. A small group of happy children can form the basis of a terrific party.

Food

Supply plenty of food and drink—children find parties hungry and thirsty work—and a variety of savory and sweet foods, both warm and cold, so that fussy guests can have a choice. Keep the food interesting with a blend of crunchy, soft and hard textures and a good mix of flavors.

When making up the menu, plan on serving four to six different savory dishes (hot and cold) plus two or three sweet dishes, including one chilled or frozen dish, plus the birthday cake. Offer two different cool drinks.

When you have chosen the menu, make a shopping list and decide which tasks can be done beforehand and what to do on the day.

Special Note

When planning party food for young children, avoid nuts and hard sweets, toothpicks and other sharp objects.

Very small children appreciate party food that is easy to hold and won't crumble or collapse. Use sturdy plastic cups and plates; they are easier for little hands to grip; half fill them to avoid spills.

At parties, toddlers will tend to 'graze', snatching a bite or two of food between play, while older kids will sit down, load their plates and speedily consume a surprising amount of food! Kids love colorful and imaginative food— especially familiar food dressed up. Cheerful napkins and tablecloths also add to the party atmosphere.

Venue

Parties don't have to be at home. Depending on the time of year, parks, zoos, amusement parks, water parks and beaches all offer alternative spaces for a party. A child's hobby could suggest a venue, such as a picnic and riding at a horse-riding school, or kite flying at the breeziest park around.

Balloons can help to make your party easy to find. For parties at home, tie a bunch of balloons and streamers to the mail box or a tree or bush.

Invitations

Party invitations can be bought or you can make your own. Write them out (or better still, let the birthday boy or girl) in colored pens on stiff paper, giving all the essential information like name, address, arrival and departure times, and theme. Give directions or include a simple map for hard-to-find places and a phone number to RSVP.

Personalized invitations are fun and easy to make. Cut out pictures or photographs from magazines of famous people, pop stars or animals. Then arrange them or glue them onto colored paper. Color or brush with glue and sprinkle with glitter.

Parties for kids aged 1 to 6

For very little ones, invite parents along as well—toddlers need help and more attention than one or two adults can give. The simplest party is an organized play time for children with phone

Kids love imaginatively presented food. (See p. 44.)

invitations. Hold the party in the backyard so there is no worry about spills. Pick a shady spot and spread out a blanket for the babies. Clean up the yard, making sure it is safe for inquisitive little people and, for your peace of mind, put anything precious out of sight and reach.

For energetic toddlers, a party lasting about two hours with five or

six guests is suitable.

Two-year-olds and under won't need organized games, preferring the sand box or toys (ensure there are plenty to go around).

For kids from four to six years, fun games can be arranged, and older children may like to help littler ones.

Parties for kids aged 7 to 12

This is the peak age for birthday parties. Older children will enjoy helping with planning and ideas, and may help with the preparation.

A garden party with around ten guests and lasting three hours will provide plenty of fun, but parties away from home save on mess and ensure plenty of space for energetic playing. Remember, girls and boys around this age often have very different ideas about what makes parties fun.

Traditional party games with balloons, balls, treasure hunts, musical chairs, etc, remain popular. If the party has a theme, adapt the food, games and prizes to match.

Keep the party moving. Make a timetable for activities and games and set aside a time for eating and for cake cutting—but don't worry if things don't go entirely as planned.

Even big kids like to take home a 'goody bag' packed with candy and toys and perhaps a piece of the birthday cake. Have extra goody bags on hand for any siblings. Keep them hidden until it's time for guests to leave.

Easy to eat and delicious savory food. (See p. 12.)

Themes

Simple ideas, such as a silly hat party or mask party, can be quite successful as full-blown themes.

Decide how much time and effort you can spare—you may like to invite all the guests to dress up and decorate a room or two, or confine your theme to the table and birthday cake.

Fancy dress-up parties are a great idea, but check with the children before you become too enthused—some kids grow out of dressing up or may feel shy. Also, making decorations or costumes can be fun, but takes time, energy and money and may be out of the question for some busy parents.

Many old favorites such as pirate or cowboy parties are still popular, yet themes are really only limited to your imagination.

Take the children to space with an Outer Limits party, featuring dressed-up aliens and astronauts and lots of 'space food'. Hold a Witch, Wizard & Warlock Convention, or host a Teddy Bears' Picnic where every child brings a bear and goes on a treasure hunt for the 'honeypot' filled with goodies. 'Bug' parties, where spiders and worms turn up in non-scary forms of drinks, cakes and meringues, are fun for younger children.

A party can be based around a movie, book or comic book, with guests dressing as their favorite characters. Little ones love to transform themselves into animals, clowns, fairies, cowboys/girls, superheroes, flowers, aliens and characters from fairy tales.

For pre-teens, set up their own disco party, featuring their current favorite pop stars and rock groups. Serve mini-burgers, hot dogs and shakes in your own 'Rock Cafe'.

If the weather is unsuitable for outdoor

entertaining, base the party around a favorite movie. Rent the movie from a video store along with old and new cartoons and play them during the party. Serve popcorn and finger foods.

Pajama parties are

fun—sleeping over is very popular; all girls or all boys being the usual rule. Set aside a large room or a tent or tents in the backyard. Make a time for lights out. Guests can bring flashlights, sleeping bags, toothbrushes, pillows and pajamas. Serve a special late-night supper of pancakes and hot chocolate.

In summer, backyard pool parties are good for older children, but all ages love to splash around in water. Under supervision, a shallow wading pool with a little water and floating toys will be a hit with toddlers.

Decorations

Adapt ideas to suit your circumstances. Party supply shops have a large range of ready-made decorations, noisemakers, helium balloons and costumes for all kinds of parties, or raid the local discount fabric store and big chains for inexpensive materials such as calico, bright cheap cottons and remnants and samples to create your decorations. Lengths of black plastic can drape a room for a spooky effect and netting comes in many colors and can be used

for everything from costumes to imitation spider webs. Crepe paper and felt are inexpensive and very adaptable for costumes and decorations.

Whatever you decide to do for your party, organize ahead and you'll be able to relax and have fun on the day.

Party Preparation

Two weeks before:

☆ Make guest list.

☆ Send out the invitations.

☆ Plan the menu. Make a list of everything you need to buy.

☆ Plan the decorations. Make a list of everything you need to buy or make.

☆ Mark on your calendar or make a timetable for preparatory tasks and do-ahead cooking.

☆ Make a timetable for the party.

☆ Recruit help.

Savory Surprises

The children's party table becomes an exciting adventure with these simply prepared and fabulous-to-eat dishes. Combine old favorites with bright new ideas, such as mini-size burgers, pizzas, spring rolls and meatballs. Tie pastry sticks up in knots, go Asian with spring rolls and satay or give guests a happy surprise with food disguised as boats. Protect the table with a bright cloth and supply plenty of napkins and good-sized, sturdy plates.

Wrapped Wieners

Preparation Time:
  20 minutes
Cooking Time:
  15–20 minutes
Makes 12

12 *cocktail wieners*
2 *sheets frozen puff
  pastry, thawed*
1 *egg, lightly beaten*
string

1 Preheat oven to 375°F. Line two baking sheets with aluminum foil. Brush with melted butter or oil.
2 Prick wieners with a fork. Roll each pastry into an 11 x 9-inch rectangle. Cut each pastry sheet into 6 rectangles (12 total). Place a wiener on each pastry rectangle at the edge; roll up. Press edge lightly to seal.
3 Carefully pinch the pastry together, about ½ inch in from edge. Tie loosely with pieces of string. Using scissors, cut a fringe from the edge almost to the string.
4 Place wrapped wieners onto the prepared baking sheet; brush lightly with the beaten egg. Bake 15–20 minutes or until golden. Remove string before serving.

HINT
For a strong display, present party food on large platters or trays. Bowls of dipping sauce can be placed directly on the platter.

Baby Burgers (top), Wrapped Wieners (bottom).

Baby Burgers

Preparation Time:
  30 minutes
Cooking Time:
  10 minutes
Makes 10

1 *pound ground beef*
1 *small onion, finely*
  chopped
1 *tablespoon finely*
  chopped parsley
1 *egg, lightly beaten*
1 *tablespoon tomato*
  sauce
½ *teaspoon garlic salt*
1 *tablespoon oil*
10 *small buns or rolls,*
  halved

Topping
2 *cups finely shredded*
  lettuce
2 *small tomatoes,*
  thinly sliced
1 *cucumber, thinly*
  sliced
5 *canned pineapple*
  rings, drained and
  halved
5 *cheese slices, halved*
tomato or barbecue
  sauce

1 Combine the ground
beef, onion, parsley,
beaten egg, tomato
sauce and garlic salt in
a large bowl. Using
hands, mix until well
combined. Divide the
mixture into 10
portions. Shape into
round patties.
2 Heat oil in a large

heavy-based pan over
medium heat. Cook the
patties 5 minutes each
side, or until they are
well browned. Remove
and drain on paper
towels.
3 To assemble burgers,
place a patty onto each
roll. Top with lettuce,
tomato, cucumber,
pineapple and cheese
slice. Top with sauce
and remaining rolls.
Serve immediately.

Kid-Style Nachos

Preparation Time:
  15 minutes
Cooking Time:
  10 minutes
Serves 6–8

6 *cups tortilla chips*
2 *cups shredded*
  cheddar cheese
2 *medium tomatoes,*
  finely chopped
2 *tablespoons finely*
  chopped green onions

1 Preheat oven to
moderate 350°F. Line a
baking sheet with foil.
2 Arrange tortilla chips
in a single layer over the
prepared baking sheet.
Sprinkle with cheese,
tomatoes and green
onion. Bake 10 minutes
or until the cheese is
melted and golden. Let
Nachos cool slightly
before serving.

Shrimp Toasts

Preparation Time:
  15 minutes
Cooking Time:
  15 minutes
Makes 32

12 *ounces medium*
  shrimp
1 *egg*
½ *teaspoon lemon*
pepper seasoning
1 *green onion, chopped*
8 *slices white bread*

1 Preheat oven to
moderate 350°F. Line
baking sheets with foil.
2 Peel and devein the
shrimp. Place shrimp,
egg, seasoning, and
green onion in food
processor bowl. Using
the pulse action, press
button 30 seconds or
until the mixture is
smooth and free of
lumps.
3 Spread evenly over
bread. Cut crusts from
bread and cut each slice
into 4 triangles. Place
onto the prepared
baking sheets. Bake 15
minutes or until golden
and slightly puffed.
Serve warm.

Note: Uncooked Shrimp
Toasts can be frozen
for 3–4 weeks.
It is not necessary to
thaw them before
cooking.

Kid-Style Nachos (top), Shrimp Toasts (bottom).

Pinwheel Kebabs

Preparation Time:
  20 minutes
Cooking Time:
  None
Makes 10

8 slices bread
1 6¾-ounce can
  boneless, skinless
  salmon, drained
1 tablespoon
  mayonnaise
2 teaspoons finely
  chopped fresh chives
apple butter
4 cheese slices
½ cup shredded
  lettuce

1 Remove crusts from
the bread. Combine the
salmon, mayonnaise
and chives in a small
mixing bowl. Stir until
smooth. Spread four
slices of bread with
salmon mixture. Roll
up the bread; cut it into
½-inch slices.
2 Spread apple butter
on the remaining bread
and top with cheese
slices and lettuce. Roll
up the bread and cut
into ½-inch slices.
3 To serve, alternately
thread the salmon and
the apple butter
pinwheels onto
skewers.

Corny Cheese Row Boats

Preparation Time:
  25 minutes
Cooking Time:
  10 minutes
Makes 6

2 tablespoons butter
2 tablespoons all-
  purpose flour
¼ cup milk
½ cup shredded
  cheddar cheese
1 7-ounce can corn
  kernels, drained
1 cup chopped cooked
  chicken
6 frozen patty shells
12 pretzel sticks

1 Bake patty shells
according to package
directions. Meanwhile,
heat butter in a
medium heavy-based
pan; add flour. Stir over
low heat for 1 minute.
2 Add milk gradually
to the pan, stirring until
smooth. Stir constantly
over medium heat for 5
minutes or until the
mixture boils and
thickens. Boil 1 minute
more; remove from
heat. Stir in the cheese,
corn and chicken.
3 Spoon mixture
evenly into shells.
Arrange pretzel sticks
as oars. Serve warm.

Corny Cheese Row Boats (top),
Pinwheel Kebabs (bottom).

1. *For Sausage Rolls: Combine sausage, onion, egg, sauces and bread crumbs.*

2. *Place a portion of meat mixture on pastry. Roll up and press edges to seal.*

Sausage Rolls

Preparation Time:
  40 minutes
Cooking Time:
  30 minutes
Makes 36

8 ounces ground pork
  sausage
1 small onion, finely
  chopped
1 egg, lightly beaten
1 tablespoon barbecue
  sauce
2 teaspoons
  Worcestershire sauce
1/3 cup fine dry bread
  crumbs
2 frozen puff pastry
  sheets, thawed
1 egg, lightly beaten,
  extra

1 Preheat oven to 350°F. Line two baking pans with aluminum foil. Brush with melted butter or oil.
2 Combine sausage, onion, egg, sauces and bread crumbs in a large bowl. Mix until well combined.
3 Cut pastry sheets in half lengthwise. Brush with extra egg. Divide sausage into 4 portions. Place one portion lengthwise down the center of each pastry sheet. Roll up and press edges to seal.
4 With the seam side down, make 9 slices in each roll, not quite cutting through. Using a long knife, carefully lift the sausage rolls onto baking pans. Brush with extra egg. Bake 30 minutes or until pastry is golden and sausage is cooked.
5 Cut into individual sausage rolls. Serve warm.

Note: Substitute ground turkey sausage or chorizo for the pork sausage, if desired.

Sausage Rolls.

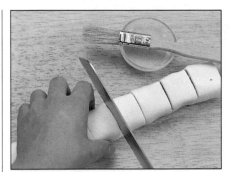

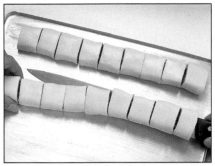

3. *Make 9 slices in each long roll, almost cutting through.*

4. *Using a long knife, lift the sausage rolls onto prepared baking pans.*

Chicken Pocket Cones

Preparation Time:
  20 minutes
Cooking Time:
  None
Makes 8

2 small round pita
  breads
3 tablespoons cheese
  spread
2 tablespoons
  mayonnaise
4 slices cooked chicken,
  halved
chives, for tying cones
1 cup shredded lettuce
1 small tomato, finely
  chopped
1 small cucumber,
  finely chopped

1 Cut each pita bread in half crosswise. Split halves horizontally to make 8 semi circles. Spread evenly with the cheese spread and the mayonnaise. Top with a slice of chicken.
2 Roll each semi circle into a cone. Tie with a chive to hold the shape.
3 Combine the lettuce, tomato and cucumber in a bowl. Fill the top of each cone with lettuce mixture. Make Chicken Pocket Cones up to 1 hour before serving. Store in refrigerator.

Cowboy Dogs

Preparation Time:
  10 minutes
Cooking Time:
  5 minutes
Makes 16

4 frankfurters
8 hot dog buns
1 8-ounce can pork and
  beans in tomato sauce
1/2 cup shredded
  cheddar cheese

1 Place frankfurters in a pan of simmering water for 3 minutes. Cut the buns in half lengthwise and hollow out the center, leaving base and sides about 1/2 inch thick.
2 Cut the frankfurters into 3/4-inch pieces; divide equally between bread shells. Cover with baked beans and sprinkle evenly with cheese. Broil until the cheese has melted and is golden brown. Leave to cool for 2 minutes before serving.

Clockwise from top: Cowboy Dogs, Ham and Pineapple Pinwheels, Chicken Pocket Cones.

Ham and Pineapple Pinwheels

Preparation Time:
  25 minutes
Cooking Time:
  15 minutes
Makes about 30

2 sheets frozen puff
  pastry, thawed
1 egg, lightly beaten
4 ounces ham, thinly
  sliced
1 8-ounce can crushed
  pineapple, drained
1/2 cup shredded
  cheddar cheese

1 Preheat oven to 350°F. Line two baking sheets with aluminum foil.
2 Lay out the pastry sheets and brush them with beaten egg. Layer each sheet with ham, pineapple and cheese. Press down gently.
3 Roll each sheet up firmly and evenly. Using a sharp serrated or electric knife, cut each roll into ten rounds. Place the pinwheels on the prepared baking sheets allowing room for spreading. Bake for 15 minutes or until golden and puffed. Serve warm.

Note: This recipe can be made up to 3 weeks in advance and stored in the freezer.

Sesame Cheese Twists and Knots

Preparation time:
10 minutes
Cooking time:
10 minutes
Makes about 24

1 sheet frozen puff
 pastry, thawed
1 egg, beaten
¼ cup finely shredded
 mozzarella cheese
1 tablespoon sesame
 seeds

1 Preheat oven to
400°F. Brush a baking
sheet with melted
butter or oil.
2 Roll out pastry sheet
until ¼ inch thick. Cut
the pastry sheet in half
lengthwise, then across
into ¾-inch strips.
3 Twist half of the
pastry strips 3 times
each, and place onto
prepared baking sheet.
Tie the remaining strips
into simple knots. Place
onto baking sheet.
4 Brush pastry lightly
with beaten egg and
sprinkle with cheese
and sesame seeds. Bake
for 10 minutes or until
puffed and golden.
Cool on a wire rack.

Note: These can be
prepared up to 3 days
in advance. Store in an
airtight container in a
cool, dry place.

HINT
For a tasty variation
on this recipe, sprinkle
pastry shapes with
poppy seeds and sea
salt. Make a sweet
version by cutting
pastry into longer
strips and forming
bows. Sprinkle with
sugar and cinnamon
and bake as above.

Sesame Cheese Twists and Knots.

*1. For Sesame Cheese Twists and Knots:
Cut the pastry into ¾-inch strips.*

*2. Twist half the strips and tie
remaining strips into simple knots.*

3. *Place the shapes onto baking sheet and brush with beaten egg.*

4. *Carefully lift cooked pastries onto a wire rack to cool.*

Mini Spring Rolls

Preparation Time:
  40 minutes
Cooking Time:
  15 minutes
Makes 16

*8 large spring roll
  wrappers
2 green onions, finely
  chopped
1/3 cup finely chopped
  green bell pepper
1/4 cup bean sprouts
6 medium shrimp,
  peeled, deveined and
  finely chopped
1 teaspoon grated
  gingerroot
2 teaspoons soy sauce
oil for deep frying
sweet and sour sauce,
  to serve*

1 Cut each wrapper in half diagonally. Cover with a damp cloth.
2 Combine the onion, bell pepper, sprouts, shrimp, gingerroot, and soy sauce in a medium mixing bowl. Stir until well combined.
3 Place 2 teaspoons of the mixture onto each wrapper at the base of triangle. Fold in edges; roll up towards point. Brush end with water; roll and press to seal.
4 Heat the oil in a deep heavy-based pan over medium-high heat to 375°F. Working in batches, gently lower

rolls into hot oil. Cook until golden and crisp. Drain on paper towels; keep warm. Repeat with remaining spring rolls. Serve warm with sweet and sour sauce for dipping.

Meatballs

Preparation time:
  15 minutes
Cooking time:
  10 minutes
Makes about 25

*12 ounces ground beef
1 small onion, finely
  chopped
1/2 cup fresh bread
  crumbs
1 tablespoon tomato
  paste
1 teaspoon
  Worcestershire sauce
1 egg, lightly beaten
2 tablespoons oil*

1 Place all ingredients except the oil in a large mixing bowl and combine. Shape level tablespoons into balls.
2 Heat oil in a large, shallow pan. Add meatballs and cook over medium heat, turning meatballs often, for 10 minutes or until beef is cooked and meatballs are evenly browned. Drain on paper towels. Serve warm.

Note: Meatballs can be cooked up to 3 days in advance. Store, covered, in the refrigerator. Reheat in a moderate 350°F oven.

Fishermen's Burgers

Preparation time:
  15 minutes
Cooking time:
  15 minutes
Makes 6

*6 frozen breaded fish
  sticks
3 slices bacon, cut in
  half (optional)
1/3 cup mayonnaise
6 dinner rolls, halved
6 small lettuce leaves
3 cheese slices, halved*

1 Preheat oven to 350°F. If desired, wrap each fish finger in a piece of bacon, tucking ends underneath. Place on a baking sheet and bake for 15 minutes or until fish stick is heated through and bacon is almost crisp. Remove and place on paper towels.
2 To assemble, spread mayonnaise on rolls. Place a lettuce leaf on bottom half of each roll. Top with cheese, a fish stick and remaining rolls. Serve warm.

*Clockwise from top: Fishermen's Burgers,
Meatballs and Mini Spring Rolls.*

Mini Pizzas

Preparation Time:
20 minutes
Cooking Time:
15 minutes
Makes 20

2 *cups all-purpose flour*
1 *teaspoon baking*
   powder
1/4 *teaspoon baking*
   soda
1/8 *teaspoon salt*
1/2 *cup butter, chopped*
1/2 *cup buttermilk*

Topping
1/3 *cup tomato or*
   spaghetti sauce
thinly sliced pepperoni
1 *small onion, sliced*
   (optional)
10 *cherry tomatoes,*
   thinly sliced
cheese slices, cut into 2-
   inch rounds

1 Preheat oven to
400°F. Line two baking
sheets with foil.
2 Place flour, baking
powder, baking soda,
salt and butter in food
processor bowl. Using
the pulse action, press
button for 30 seconds
or until mixture is a
fine crumbly texture.
Add buttermilk,
process for 30 seconds
or until the mixture
comes together. Knead
dough gently on a
lightly floured surface
until smooth.
3 Roll the dough out

to 1/4-inch thickness.
Cut into rounds using a
3-inch cutter. Place
onto baking sheets.
4 Spread sauce evenly
over dough rounds.
Arrange the pepperoni,
onion (if using) and
tomato slices evenly
over sauce; top with
cheese. Bake for 15
minutes or until crisp.
Serve warm.

Note: Mini Pizzas can
be made up to 3 weeks
ahead. Freeze uncooked;
bake without thawing.

Ham and Cheese Balls

Preparation Time:
   10 minutes
Cooking Time:
   None
Makes about 24

1/2 *cup sesame seeds*
4 *ounces soft cream*
   cheese
4 *ounces ham, finely*
   chopped
1/4 *cup shredded*
   cheddar cheese

1 Spread sesame seeds
in a shallow baking
pan. Broil 4 to 5 inches
from heat for a few
seconds or until golden.
Cool; set aside.
2 Place cream cheese in

a medium mixing bowl
and mash with a fork.
Add the ham and
cheese; mix to
combine. Using hands,
roll heaping teaspoons
of mixture into balls.
3 Roll balls in sesame
seeds. Refrigerate for 1
hour before serving.

Avocado Dip

Preparation time:
   10 minutes
Cooking time:
   None
Makes about 1 cup

8 *ounces soft cream*
   cheese
2 *small ripe avocados*
1 *tablespoon lemon*
   juice
1/4 *teaspoon onion*
   powder
cayenne pepper
tortilla chips, to serve
mixed vegetable sticks,
   to serve

1 Place cream cheese in
a medium mixing bowl.
Peel and pit avocados.
Mash flesh and add to
cheese with lemon
juice, onion powder
and cayenne pepper to
taste. Combine well.
2 Cover and place in
refrigerator until ready
to serve. Serve chilled
with tortilla chips and
mixed vegetable sticks.

Clockwise from top: Mini Pizzas, Ham and
Cheese Balls and Avocado Dip.

Chicken Nuggets

Preparation Time:
  20 minutes
Cooking Time:
  15 minutes
Makes 34

12 ounces boneless
  skinless chicken thighs,
  coarsely chopped
1 egg, lightly beaten
1 tablespoon chopped
  fresh chives
1/4 teaspoon sesame oil
1 tablespoon plum
  sauce
1 teaspoon soy sauce
1 cup cornflake crumbs
sweet and sour sauce or
  extra plum sauce, for
  dipping

1 Preheat oven to
375°F. Line a baking
sheet with foil. Brush
with melted butter or
oil.
2 Process chicken,
beaten egg, chives,
sesame oil and sauces
using the pulse action
for 40 seconds or until
smooth.
3 Shape heaping
teaspoons of mixture
into balls. Roll in
crumbs. Place onto
prepared baking sheet.
Bake for 15 minutes or
until golden and
chicken cooked. Serve
hot with sauce for
dipping.

Chicken Nuggets (left), Cheese and
Bacon Tarts (right).

Note: Nuggets can be
prepared and cooked
up to 3 weeks in
advance. Cool and
freeze in an airtight
container. Reheat just
before serving.

Cheese and Bacon Tarts

Preparation Time:
  30 minutes
Cooking Time:
  20 minutes
Makes 12

1 15-ounce package
  refrigerated unbaked
  piecrust (2 crusts)
3 slices bacon, crisp-
  cooked and crumbled
1/4 cup finely chopped
  onion (optional)
2/3 cup light cream
1 egg
1/2 teaspoon yellow
  mustard
1/3 cup shredded
  cheddar cheese

1 Preheat oven to
350°F. Brush 12 muffin
cups with melted butter
or oil.
2 Lay out pastry on a
lightly floured surface.
Cut out 12 rounds with
a 4-inch fluted cutter.
Ease them into muffin
cups. Sprinkle on the
bacon and onion (if
using).

3 Combine cream, egg
and mustard; whisk
until smooth. Divide
mixture between pastry
shells. Sprinkle with
cheese. Bake 20 minutes
or until a knife inserted
in the center comes out
clean. Serve warm.

Note: You can
substitute 1/4 cup
drained and flaked
canned tuna for the
cooked bacon.

Zebra Sandwiches

Preparation time:
  10 minutes
Cooking time:
  None
Makes 8 small
  sandwiches

4 slices bread
1 tablespoon softened
  butter
2 tablespoons apple
  butter or hazelnut
  spread

1 Spread 3 slices of
bread with butter and
either of the spreads.
Stack slices, spread side
up. Top with the plain
slice. Press down
gently.
2 Cut crusts neatly
from bread. Cut the
stack in half to make
rectangles, then slice
each crosswise into
four Zebra Sandwiches.

Tiny Tuna Baskets

Preparation time:
  15 minutes
Cooking time:
  15 minutes
Makes 24

*6 slices stale white
  bread
2 tablespoons butter,
  melted
1 3¹/₄-ounce can water-
  pack tuna
¹/₄ cup cheese spread
1 tablespoon chopped
  fresh parsley
6 cherry tomatoes,
  quartered*

1 Preheat oven to 350°F.
2 Remove crusts from bread. Flatten slices with a rolling pin; brush each side lightly with melted butter. Cut each slice into quarters. Press into 24 miniature muffin cups. Bake for 15 minutes or until crisp and golden. Cool.
3 Place undrained tuna in a bowl. Add cheese spread and parsley and combine well. Just before serving, place a teaspoon of mixture in each shell. Garnish with tomato.

Note: The bread shells can be made up to one week ahead. Store in an airtight container.

Chicken Satay with Peanut Sauce

Preparation time:
  15 minutes
Cooking time:
  10 minutes
Makes 12

*1 pound boneless
  skinless chicken
  breasts, thinly sliced
1 tablespoon oil
1 tablespoon honey
1 tablespoon soy sauce*

Peanut Sauce
*¹/₂ cup smooth peanut
  butter
1 tablespoon soy sauce
¹/₂ cup water
1 teaspoon sugar
1 teaspoon sweet chili
  sauce (optional)*

1 Thread chicken onto skewers. Combine oil, honey and soy sauce and brush over chicken. Place chicken on lightly oiled broiler pan. Broil 3 to 4 inches from heat for 10 minutes or until tender; turn and brush with oil mixture several times.
2 Serve warm with Peanut Sauce.
3 To make Peanut Sauce, place all ingredients in a small pan. Stir over medium heat until smooth.

Clockwise from top: Chicken Satay with Peanut Sauce, Tiny Tuna Baskets and Zebra Sandwiches (p. 23).

Savory Phyllo Rolls

Preparation time:
20 minutes
Cooking time:
15 minutes
Makes 12

1 *small onion, finely*
chopped
1 *pound lean ground*
beef
2 *tablespoons tomato*
paste
1 *teaspoon dried*
Italian seasoning or
basil, crushed
1/4 *teaspoon salt*
12 *sheets frozen phyllo*
dough, thawed
1/3 *cup butter, melted*

1 Preheat oven to
375°F. Brush a baking
sheet with melted
butter or oil.
2 In a saucepan cook
beef and onion until
meat is well browned.
Drain and break up
any lumps. Stir in
tomato paste, seasoning
or basil and salt.
3 Place 1 sheet of
phyllo dough onto the
work surface. Brush
half with melted butter
and fold over
unbuttered half. Place 2
heaping tablespoons
meat mixture ¾ inch
from front edge. Roll
over once, fold sides in
and roll to end. Brush
with melted butter.
Repeat with remaining
ingredients.
4 Place onto baking
sheet. Bake 15–20
minutes till crisp and
golden. Serve warm.

Mini Chicken Pastries

Preparation time:
20 minutes
Cooking time:
15 minutes
Makes 18

8 *ounces ground*
chicken or turkey
1/4 *cup finely chopped*
onion
1/2 *teaspoon lemon*
pepper seasoning
2 *sheets frozen puff*
pastry, thawed
1 *egg, beaten*

1 Preheat oven to
400°F. Brush a baking
sheet with melted
butter or oil.
2 Cook chicken or
turkey and onion in a
saucepan until no
longer pink; break up
any lumps. Remove
from heat; drain. Stir in
seasoning.
3 Lay out pastry on a
lightly floured surface.
Cut into rounds with a
3-inch cutter. Place a
scant tablespoon of
mixture onto each.
Fold rounds in half,
press edges together.
Place onto baking sheet
and brush lightly with
beaten egg. Bake for 15
minutes or until
golden.

Note: Mini Chicken
Pastries can be cooked
and frozen for up to 2
months. Thaw in the
refrigerator; reheat in a
warm oven 10 minutes.

Bologna Swags

Preparation time:
15 minutes
Cooking time:
None
Makes 12

6 *slices whole wheat*
bread
6 *cheese sticks*
6 *slices bologna*
12 *chives*
spaghetti sauce, to
serve

1 Remove crusts from
bread and flatten. Place
a slice of bologna on
each. Place a cheese
stick close to one edge.
Roll up tightly.
2 Tie 2 chives around
each roll, a quarter of
the way in from each
of the ends.
3 Cut rolls in half so
that the tie is in the
center of each Swag.
Serve with spaghetti
sauce for dipping.

Clockwise from top left: Mini Chicken Pastries,
Savory Phyllo Rolls and Bologna Swags.

Sweet Things

Among this selection of delightful birthday treats, sweets, small cakes, bars and cookies you'll be sure to find just the right dishes to complement your other party fare. Many children think chocolates and cakes are the yummiest things about birthday parties and will eat them exclusively. To avoid this, serve the savory foods first, then bring out the sweets. Remember to serve the drinks, too.

Martians

Preparation Time:
  15 minutes
Cooking Time:
  15 minutes
Makes 24

½ *cup butter*
⅔ *cup sugar*
1 *egg*
2 *cups all-purpose flour*

Icing
1 *cup powdered sugar,*
  sifted
3–4 *teaspoons hot*
  water
4 *drops green food*
  coloring
assorted candy

1 Using electric beaters, beat butter, sugar and egg until light and creamy.
2 Add flour; beat until well combined. Turn onto a lightly floured surface, knead 2 minutes till smooth.
3 Preheat oven to 350°F. On a lightly floured surface roll dough to ¼-inch thickness. Cut into shapes using a 3-inch gingerbread man cutter. Place on baking sheets. Bake 15 minutes or till lightly golden. Cool on wire rack.
4 Drizzle the front of each cookie with icing; spread to evenly coat. While icing is still soft, decorate with candy. Un-iced cookies can be made up to 7 days ahead. Store iced cookies up to 2 days in an airtight container.
5 To make Icing: Combine powdered sugar, water and food coloring in a medium bowl and stir until smooth.

Chocolate Haystacks (p. 30) (top), Martians (bottom).

Chocolate Haystacks

Preparation Time:
15 minutes
Cooking Time:
10 minutes
Makes 40

2 cups sugar
⅓ cup unsweetened
  cocoa powder
½ cup milk
½ cup butter, chopped
3 cups rolled oats
1½ cups shredded or
  flaked coconut

1 Combine sugar and cocoa powder in a large heavy-based pan. Add milk and butter. Stir over low heat without boiling until butter has melted and sugar has completely dissolved. Bring the mixture to a full rolling boil, stirring constantly; remove from heat immediately. Add the oats and coconut; combine well.
2 Working quickly, drop heaping teaspoons of mixture onto a baking sheet or tray lined with waxed paper. Allow to set. Store in an airtight container in a cool, dry place.

Note: For easier handling, spoon the hot mixture into paper muffin cups.

Orange Fairy Cakes

Preparation Time:
25 minutes
Cooking Time:
10 minutes
*Makes 18 large or
36 miniature*

½ cup butter
1¼ cups sugar
2 eggs, lightly beaten
orange food coloring
orange extract
2 cups all-purpose
  flour
¼ teaspoon ground
  nutmeg
⅔ cup milk

Icing
4 ounces cream cheese
½ cup powdered sugar,
  sifted
2 teaspoons grated
  orange peel
1 teaspoon honey
1 teaspoon orange
  juice

1 Preheat oven to 350°F. Line 18 regular or 36 miniature muffin cups with paper bake cups.
2 Using electric beaters, beat butter and sugar until light and creamy. Add eggs gradually, beating thoroughly after each addition. Add a few drops of food coloring and extract; beat until just combined.
3 Transfer the mixture to a large mixing bowl. Using a metal spoon, fold in the flour and nutmeg alternately with milk. Stir until just combined and mixture is smooth.
4 Fill muffin cups ⅔ full. Bake 18 minutes for regular or 10 minutes for miniature cupcakes or until a toothpick inserted in the center comes out clean.
5 Let cupcakes cool in muffin pans for 5 minutes before turning onto a wire rack to cool. When cool, spread Icing on cakes. Store un-iced cupcakes in the freezer for up to 4 weeks. Iced cupcakes will keep up to 2 days in an airtight container.
6 To make Icing: Beat cream cheese until soft and creamy. Add the remaining ingredients, beating for 3 minutes or until the mixture is smooth and fluffy.

Orange Fairy Cakes.

Peanut Butter Fudge

Preparation Time:
 15 minutes
Cooking Time:
 25 minutes
Makes 36 pieces

2 cups sugar
3/4 cup milk
2 tablespoons light
 corn syrup
1/4 cup peanut butter
1 teaspoon vanilla

1 Line an 8 x 8 x 2-inch baking pan with aluminum foil; brush with melted butter or oil.
2 Combine sugar, milk and corn syrup in a heavy-based pan. Stir in peanut butter over medium heat until sugar dissolves. Brush sugar crystals from sides of pan with a wet pastry brush. Clip candy thermometer to side of pan. Bring to a boil and reduce heat slightly. Cook, stirring frequently, until thermometer registers 234°F, soft-ball stage. Remove from heat.
3 Add vanilla; do not stir. Let mixture cool to 110°F. Remove thermometer. Using a wooden spoon, beat until very thick and glossy. Pour into pan. Cut into squares when set.

Mini Berry Muffins

Preparation Time:
 30 minutes
Cooking Time:
 10 minutes
Makes 44 muffins

2 cups all-purpose flour
2 teaspoons baking
 powder
1/4 teaspoon salt
1/4 teaspoon baking
 soda
1/2 teaspoon grated
 orange peel
1/2 cup brown sugar
1 cup milk
1 egg, lightly beaten
1/3 cup butter, melted
1 cup fresh or frozen, or
 one 3-ounce package
 dried blueberries

1 Preheat oven to 350°F. Line miniature muffin cups with paper bake cups or lightly grease.
2 Combine flour, baking powder, salt baking soda, orange peel and sugar. Make a well in the center. Add combined milk, egg and butter. Using a wooden spoon, stir well; do not overbeat.
3 Lightly fold berries into the mixture. Spoon tablespoons of mixture into muffin cups. Bake 10 minutes or until golden.

4 Let muffins stand 5 minutes before cooling on wire rack. Store in an airtight container in a cool, dry place for up to 3 days or freeze for several weeks.

Wiggly Fruit Shapes

Preparation Time:
 15 minutes + 1 hour
 refrigeration
Cooking Time:
 5 minutes
Serves 6–8

2 cups orange juice
1/4 cup sugar
2 envelopes unflavored
 gelatin

1 Line a 9 x 9 x 2-inch baking dish with aluminum foil. Brush or spray with oil.
2 Combine juice and sugar in heavy-based pan. Sprinkle with gelatin. Stir over low heat until they have dissolved. Bring to a boil; boil 1 minute. Remove from heat. Pour mixture into prepared dish. (Strain if lumpy.) Refrigerate at least 1 hour till set.
3 Turn gelatin out of pan. Remove foil; cut a variety of shapes using cookie cutters. Chill till ready to serve.
Note: Make different Wiggly Fruit Shapes using raspberry or grape juices.

Clockwise from left: Peanut Butter Fudge, Mini Berry Muffins and Wiggly Fruit Shapes.

Pretty Party Stars

Preparation Time:
  30 minutes
Cooking Time:
  10 minutes
Makes 60

½ *cup butter, softened*
½ *cup sugar*
1 *egg, lightly beaten*
2 *tablespoons honey*
2 *teaspoons grated lemon peel*
2¼ *cups all-purpose flour*
½ *teaspoon ground ginger*

Icing
2 *cups powdered sugar, sifted*
2–3 *tablespoons lemon juice*
silver dragees, to decorate

1 Preheat oven to moderate 350°F.
2 Using electric beaters, beat butter and sugar in small mixing bowl until the mixture is light and creamy. Add the beaten egg and beat well. Add the honey and lemon peel; beat until combined.
3 Transfer mixture to a large mixing bowl. Using a metal spoon, fold in the combined flour and ginger. Stir to form a stiff dough.
4 Roll dough between two sheets of plastic wrap or on a lightly floured surface to ¼-inch thickness. Cut the dough into stars with a 2-inch cutter. Place cookie dough stars on baking sheets. Bake the cookies for 10 minutes or until firm and pale golden. Let cookies cool on baking sheets for 5 minutes before transferring them to a wire rack to cool. When cool, spread them with Icing using a small metal spatula and decorate with the silver dragees. Store Pretty Party Stars in an airtight container between sheets of waxed paper in a cool, dry place for up to 7 days.
5 To make Icing: Stir together the sifted powdered sugar and just enough of the lemon juice to make a smooth, spreadable glaze.

HINT
Most children love to eat candy, but if there is a reason for sugar not being allowed try these alternatives: dried apples, apricots, mixed fruit bits or banana chips; small boxes of raisins; chopped dates. Older children enjoy shelling peanuts, walnuts, almonds and pistachios.

Pretty Party Stars.

1. *For Pretty Party Stars: Add honey and peel to batter; beat to combine.*

2. *Using a metal spoon, fold in combined flour and ground ginger.*

3. Roll out pastry and cut into stars with a 2-inch cutter.

4. Using a small metal spatula, spread cookies with icing.

Cornflake Crunchies

Preparation Time:
  20 minutes
Cooking Time:
  10 minutes
Makes 18

¹/₃ cup butter
¹/₄ cup honey
¹/₄ cup packed brown
  sugar
3 cups cornflakes
¹/₄ cup chopped
  candied cherries or dates
2 tablespoons chopped
  mixed nuts (optional)

1 Line 18 muffin cups with paper bake cups.
2 Combine the butter, honey and sugar in a small heavy-based pan. Stir over low heat without boiling until the butter has melted and sugar is completely dissolved. Bring to a boil; reduce heat. Simmer for 5 minutes. Remove from heat immediately.
3 Combine cornflakes, cherries or dates, nuts (if using) and butter mixture in a medium mixing bowl. Spoon the mixture into muffin cups. Refrigerate until set, about 1 hour. Store in an airtight container in refrigerator for up to 5 days.

Beach Babies

Preparation Time:
  20 minutes + 1 hour
  refrigeration
Cooking Time:
  None
Makes 8

1 3-ounce package
  blueberry-flavored
  gelatin
1 cup boiling water
12 gummy bear candies
2 tablespoons finely
  crushed vanilla wafers
8 fruit-flavored circle
  candies
12 miniature paper
  umbrellas

1 Line 8 muffin cups with a double layer of paper bake cups.
2 In a 2-cup glass measure stir gelatin and water till gelatin dissolves. Stand till cool, but not set.
3 Pour into muffin cups until ³/₄ full. Refrigerate at least 1 hour till set.
4 Sprinkle the crushed cookie crumbs over half of each gelatin cup. Lay a gummy bear on the crumbs. Lean a circle candy against the edge of bake cup and an umbrella in the center. Serve immediately.
Note: Use lime-flavored gelatin if blueberry is not available.

Cornflake Crunchies (left), Beach Babies (right).

Smiling Pancake Faces

Preparation Time:
  10 minutes
Cooking Time:
  15 minutes
Makes 10–14

1½ *cups pancake mix*
2 *ounces semisweet*
  chocolate, chopped
oil

1 Prepare pancake mix according to package directions. Leave to stand for 10 minutes.
2 Meanwhile, place chocolate in a small heatproof bowl or top of a double boiler. Place over a pan of simmering water. Stir until chocolate melts and is smooth. Spoon chocolate into a small paper piping bag (see Hint), seal open end. Snip tip off bag.

3 Lightly oil skillet or griddle and place over medium heat. Pipe a small face with the chocolate in the bottom of skillet or on griddle. Spoon enough pancake batter over face to cover. Cook until bubbles appear on the surface and underside is golden brown. Turn and cook other side.
4 Remove from pan; repeat with remaining ingredients. Serve warm or cold.

Hint
To make an icing bag, cut a 10-inch square of waxed or parchment paper. Fold in half into a triangle. With the long side at the bottom roll a corner to the center and tape in place. Wrap the other side around the back and tape in place.

Smiling Pancake Faces.

1. For *Smiling Pancake Faces:* Make pancake mix according to directions.

2. Make a small paper icing bag, spoon chocolate in and seal.

3. Pipe a small face with the chocolate onto the base of the pan.

4. Working quickly, spoon enough batter to cover the face.

Chocolate Chip Shortbread

Preparation Time:
  30 minutes
Cooking Time:
  35– 40 minutes
Makes 30

1 *cup butter, softened*
¾ *cup powdered sugar*
2 *tablespoons chocolate-*
  flavored drink mix
2 *cups all-purpose flour*
½ *cup milk*
½ *cup semisweet*
  chocolate chips
semisweet chocolate
  chips, extra

1 Preheat oven to 300°F.
2 Using electric beaters, beat butter and sugar until light and creamy. Add chocolate drink mix; beat until combined.
3 Transfer mixture to a large mixing bowl. Using a metal spoon, fold in the flour alternately with the milk. Stir until just combined and mixture is almost smooth. Add ½ cup chocolate chips. Using floured hands, roll tablespoons of the mixture into balls. Place on baking sheets. Place extra chocolate chips on balls of dough. Bake 35–40 minutes or until firm. Let cool 5 minutes on baking sheets before transferring to wire racks to cool.

Gelatin Sandwiches

Preparation Time:
  15 minutes + 1 hour
  refrigeration
Cooking Time:
  None
Makes 18–20

2 *3-ounce packages*
  strawberry-flavored
  gelatin
2 *cups boiling water*
thin wafer cookies or
  graham crackers

1 Line an 11 x 7 x 2 or 9 x 9 x 2-inch baking pan with aluminum foil. Brush or spray with oil.
2 In a bowl stir gelatin and water until the gelatin dissolves. Pour into baking pan. Refrigerate at least 1 hour till set.
3 Using foil, lift gelatin from pan. Peel foil back from sides of gelatin and cut to fit wafers or graham crackers. Sandwich gelatin between 2 wafers or graham crackers.
Note: Do not refrigerate assembled Sandwiches because the wafers or graham crackers will soften.

Gelatin Sandwiches (top), Chocolate Chip Shortbread (bottom).

Chocolate Chip Crackles

Preparation Time:
  20 minutes
Cooking Time:
  5 minutes
Makes 24

3 cups crisp rice cereal
1/4 cup unsweetened
  cocoa powder
1 1/2 cups powdered
  sugar
1/2 cup raisins
1 cup flaked coconut
2/3 cup butter
1/2 cup chocolate chips

1 Line 24 muffin cups
with paper bake cups.
Place cereal in large
mixing bowl. Add
cocoa powder,
powdered sugar, raisins
and coconut. Stir until
well combined.
2 Place butter in small
pan. Heat gently until
melted; stir into mixture
with chocolate chips.
3 Spoon about 1/4 cup
cereal mixture into
each muffin cup.
Refrigerate until set.
Store in airtight
container in refrigerator
for up to 5 days.

Tiny Strawberry Tarts

Preparation Time:
  20 minutes
Cooking Time:
  20 minutes
Makes 24

2/3 cup all-purpose flour
3 tablespoons butter
1 tablespoon sugar
2–3 tablespoons water
1 4-serving size
  package instant
  vanilla pudding mix
12 small strawberries,
  halved
2 tablespoons apple
  jelly

1 Place flour and
butter in a medium
mixing bowl. Using
fingertips or pastry
blender, rub butter into
the flour until mixture
is a fine, crumbly
texture. Stir in the
sugar. Add almost all
the water. Mix to a
firm dough, adding
more water if
necessary. Turn the
dough onto a lightly
floured surface and
knead for 2 minutes or
until smooth.
2 Preheat oven to
moderate 350°F. On a
lightly floured surface
roll the pastry out to
1/8-inch thickness. Cut
the pastry into rounds

using a 2-inch cutter.
Press the rounds into
miniature muffin pans
and bake for 15
minutes or until lightly
golden. Set them aside
to cool.
3 Meanwhile, prepare
the instant vanilla

*Tiny Strawberry Tarts and
Chocolate Chip Crackles.*

pudding mix according to package directions.
4 To assemble the Tiny Strawberry Tarts, place a teaspoon of vanilla pudding into each pastry shell. Top with half a strawberry and brush with warmed apple jelly.

Use the remaining pudding as desired.
Note: Pastry shells cases can be made up to 7 days ahead and stored in an airtight container.
The pudding can be made up to

24 hours in advance and stored in the refrigerator in an air tight container.
Tiny Strawberry Tarts can be assembled up to four hours before serving. Store in refrigerator.

Rainbow Cupcakes

Preparation Time:
20 minutes + 1 hour
refrigeration
Cooking Time:
15–20 minutes
Makes 24–28

1 package 2-layer
yellow cake mix
1 3-ounce package
strawberry- or cherry-
flavored gelatin
1 3-ounce package
lime-flavored gelatin
1²/₃ cups boiling water
2 cups shredded
coconut

1 Lightly grease 24–28
muffin cups; set aside.
2 Prepare cake mix
according to package
directions, following
instructions to make
cupcakes. Fill muffin
cups ²/₃ full. Bake
according to package
directions. Remove
from muffin cups and
cool on a wire rack.
3 Place gelatin into
separate small mixing
bowls. Pour half the
boiling water into each
bowl and stir until
gelatin dissolves. Allow
to cool, but not set.
4 Working one at a
time, dip each cupcake
into either green or red
gelatin, then roll in the
coconut. Place coated

cupcakes on a plate or
tray to set. Repeat with
remaining cakes.
Refrigerate at least 1
hour to set. Serve
chilled.

Colorful Fairy Bread

Preparation Time:
10 minutes
Cooking Time:
None
Serves 8

8 slices white bread
2–3 tablespoons butter,
softened
colored sprinkles

1 Spread one side of
bread with butter and
remove crusts. Place a
cookie cutter in the
center of the slice as a
guide. Sprinkle a light,
even coating of one
color of sprinkles inside
the guide, and a
contrasting color on
the outside.
2 Remove cutter; press
sprinkles gently with
fingers to secure. Fairy
bread can be made up
to 2 hours ahead. Store
in refrigerator.

Note: Spirals or stripes
of colored sprinkles are
also very effective.

*Colorful Fairy Bread (left),
Rainbow Cupcakes (right).*

Meringue Snails and Worms

Preparation Time:
  30 minutes
Cooking Time:
  35 minutes
Makes about 30

2 egg whites
1/2 cup sugar
2 tablespoons
  powdered sugar
2 teaspoons lemon juice
food coloring, optional
colored sprinkles,
  optional
candy, optional

1 Preheat oven to slow 300°F. Brush 2 baking sheets with melted butter or oil. Line with paper; grease paper. Dust lightly with sifted cornstarch; shake off excess.
2 Place egg whites in a small, dry mixing bowl. Using electric beaters, beat the whites until soft peaks form.
3 Add sugar gradually, beating constantly until mixture is thick and glossy. Add powdered sugar, lemon juice and a few drops of food coloring, if using. Beat 3 minutes more or until all the sugar is dissolved.
4 Spoon mixture into a large piping bag, fitted with a plain round nozzle; pipe worm and snail shapes onto the prepared baking sheets. Decorate shapes with sprinkles or use candy for eyes and teeth. Bake 35 minutes or until pale and crisp. Remove from the oven; cool on baking sheets. Store meringues, lightly packed or in a single layer, in an airtight container in a cool, dry place for up to 3 weeks.

Cherry and Coconut Squares

Preparation Time:
  30 minutes
Cooking Time:
  25–30 minutes
Makes 20 squares

2 eggs, separated
2/3 cup powdered sugar
1 cup flaked coconut
1/4 cup chopped
  candied cherries or
  dates
1/2 cup ground almonds
3 tablespoons all-
  purpose flour
2 teaspoons grated
  lemon peel
1/4 cup shredded
  coconut, extra

1 Preheat oven to moderate 350°F. Brush an 8 x 8 x 2-inch baking pan with melted butter or oil. Line base and sides with paper; grease paper.
2 Place egg whites in small, dry mixing bowl. Using electric beaters, beat egg whites until soft peaks form.
3 Add sugar gradually, beating 5 minutes or until mixture is thick. Add yolks; beat 3 minutes more.
4 Transfer mixture to a large mixing bowl. Using a metal spoon, fold in the coconut, cherries or dates, almonds, flour and lemon peel. Stir until just combined and the mixture is almost smooth.
5 Spoon mixture into prepared pan; smooth surface. Sprinkle with extra coconut. Bake 25–30 minutes or until golden brown and a toothpick inserted near the center comes out clean. Let stand 5 minutes in pan before turning onto a wire rack to cool. When cool, cut into squares with a sharp knife. Store in an airtight container in a cool, dry place for up to 2 weeks.

Note: Replace cherries or dates with other dried fruit, if desired.

Meringue Snails and Worms (top), Cherry and Coconut Squares (bottom).

Popcorn Pops

Preparation Time:
15 minutes
Cooking Time:
10 minutes
Makes 6

6 cups popped popcorn
1 cup sugar
1/2 cup water
1/2 cup light corn syrup
4 drops red or green
  food coloring
6 wooden popsicle
  sticks

1 Put popcorn in a
large bowl; set aside.
2 Combine the sugar,
water and corn syrup
in a heavy-based pan.
Stir over medium heat
without boiling until
sugar has completely
dissolved. Brush sugar
crystals from the sides
of the pan with a wet
pastry brush. Bring to a
boil. Boil without
stirring for 5 minutes.
Remove from heat; stir
in food coloring.
3 Pour the syrup
mixture over the
popcorn. Using two
metal spoons, combine
thoroughly. Allow the
mixture to cool until
just possible to handle.
With oiled hands and
working quickly, press
the popcorn firmly into
rough ball shapes
around the top of each
popsicle stick. Wrap

each ball of popcorn in
clear plastic wrap.
Serve the same day.

Marshmallow Bars

Preparation Time:
10 minutes
Cooking Time:
5 minutes
Makes 32

3 cups crisp rice cereal
26 large marshmallows,
  chopped
1 cup flaked coconut
1/2 cup butter
4 ounces semisweet
  chocolate, chopped

1 Line a 9 x 9 x 2-inch
baking dish with
aluminum foil.
Combine the cereal,
marshmallows and
coconut in a large
mixing bowl.
2 Place butter in a
small pan and stir over
a low heat until melted.
Add to cereal mixture.
Using a wooden spoon,
stir until combined.
Pour into the prepared
pan. Cover and chill
until set.
3 Place chocolate in a
small heatproof bowl
or top of double boiler.
Place over a pan of
simmering water; stir
until chocolate is
melted and smooth.

Let cool slightly; pour
over marshmallow and
cereal mixture. Spread
chocolate evenly with a
small metal spatula.
Chill until set. Lift out
of pan with foil and
remove foil; cut into
bars.

Chocolate Dip

Preparation Time:
5 minutes
Cooking Time:
None
Makes about 2 cups

8 ounces vanilla yogurt
8 ounces soft-style
  cream cheese
1/2 cup chocolate syrup
chopped fruit, to serve,
marshmallows, to serve

1 Combine yogurt and
cream cheese in a
medium bowl. Using a
wooden spoon or
electric beaters, beat
until mixture is smooth
and free of lumps.
2 Add chocolate syrup;
stir or beat until well
combined. Transfer to a
serving bowl. Serve
with small pieces of
seasonal fruit and
marshmallows.
Chocolate Dip can be
made up to 24 hours in
advance. Store in the
refrigerator and stir
before serving.

From top: Marshmallow Bars, Popcorn
Pops and Chocolate Dip.

49

Crunchy-Top Brownies

Preparation Time:
 15 minutes
Cooking Time:
 30 minutes
Makes 16

1¼ cups all-purpose
 flour
5 ounces semisweet
 chocolate, chopped
2 tablespoons water
½ cup butter
½ cup sugar
2 eggs, lightly beaten
⅓ cup chocolate-
 flavored crisp rice
 cereal

Icing
1 cup powdered sugar,
 sifted
½ cup butter,
 softened

1 Preheat oven to
350°F. Brush an 8 x 8 x
2-inch baking pan with
melted butter or oil.
2 Place flour in a large
mixing bowl. Make a
well in the center.
Combine chocolate,
water and butter in a
small pan. Stir over low
heat until chocolate
and butter have melted.
Add sugar and stir until
sugar dissolves; remove
from heat; cool.

3 Add chocolate
mixture and beaten
eggs to dry ingredients.
Using a wooden spoon,
stir until combined; do
not overbeat.
4 Pour mixture into
prepared pan. Bake 30
minutes. Cool in pan.
5 Ice cooled brownies;
sprinkle with cereal;
cut into squares. Store
in an airtight container
in the refrigerator.
6 To make Icing:
Combine the sugar and
butter; beat until smooth.

Pink Marshmallows

Preparation Time:
 25 minutes +
 overnight setting
Cooking Time:
 None
Makes 36

1¾ cups sugar
⅔ cup water
2 envelopes unflavored
 gelatin
½ cup water, extra
1 teaspoon vanilla
4 drops red food
 coloring
1 cup powdered sugar

1 Line a 13 x 9 x 2-
inch baking pan with
foil; brush with melted
butter or oil.

2 Using electric
beaters, beat sugar and
water for 3 minutes.
3 Combine the gelatin
with water in a bowl.
Stand bowl in hot
water; stir until gelatin
dissolves. Add to sugar
mixture. Using electric
beaters, beat for 10
minutes, till mixture is

Pink Marshmallows (left), Crunchy-Top Brownies (right).

thick and white. Add vanilla and red food coloring and beat.
4 Pour the mixture into prepared pan and spread evenly. Cover loosely with plastic wrap and let stand overnight at room temperature.
5 Turn marshmallow out of pan, peel off foil; cut into squares. Place powdered sugar in a plastic bag; add a few cubes of marshmallow at a time; shake to coat with powdered sugar. Store in an airtight container in a cool, dark place for up to 1 week.

HINT
In hot weather, even the most dedicated anti-washers among young guests will appreciate a wet cloth to clean up sticky little hands and faces. Purchased wet paper cloths are convenient.

Icy Treats & Drinks

Being a guest at a children's party can be hot and thirsty work, so refreshing drinks and chilled desserts are always welcome. Offer guests a choice of two drinks; for example, our tasty, thirst-quenching Homemade Lemonade and a more substantial creamy one such as Choc-Chip Banana Smoothies. Dress up ice-cream cones, parfaits and sundaes in their party best to please young eyes and palates, too. Serve dishes straight from freezer or refrigerator; keep portions small to suit kid-size appetites.

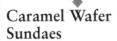

Caramel Wafer Sundaes

Preparation Time:
  20 minutes
Cooking Time:
  5 minutes
Serves 8

16 scoops vanilla ice cream
4 oblong sandwich cookie wafers
2 choc-coated caramel fudge bars, chopped

Caramel Sauce
1/2 cup packed brown sugar
1 tablespoon cornstarch
1/4 cup water
1/3 cup light cream
2 tablespoons light corn syrup
1 tablespoon butter

1 To make Caramel Sauce: Combine the brown sugar and cornstarch in a small heavy-based pan. Stir in water. Stir in cream and corn syrup. Cook and stir until bubbly. Cook 2 minutes more. Remove from heat; stir in butter.
2 Place 2 scoops of ice cream into each bowl. Pour Caramel Sauce over. Decorate with cookie wafers cut into triangles and the chopped fudge bars.

Note: Caramel Sauce can be made up to 2 weeks in advance. Store the sauce in an airtight container in the refrigerator. Reheat gently before serving.

Caramel Wafer Sundaes (left), Choc-Chip Banana Smoothies (p. 54) (right).

Choc-Chip Banana Smoothie

Preparation Time:
 10 minutes
Cooking Time:
 None
Makes 4 cups

1 cup milk
2 large ripe bananas
1/2 cup vanilla yogurt
1 cup vanilla ice cream
2 tablespoons chocolate
 syrup
1 tablespoon honey
1/2 cup chocolate chips
grated semisweet or
 milk chocolate, to
 garnish
chocolate chips, to
 garnish

1 Place the milk, bananas, yogurt, ice cream, chocolate syrup, honey and chocolate chips together in food processor bowl. Using the pulse action press button and process 30 seconds or until the mixture is fairly smooth.
2 Pour the mixture into clear plastic cups. Serve right away or store, covered, in the refrigerator for up to 3 hours.
Just before serving, sprinkle the smoothies with grated chocolate and additional chocolate chips.

Sunburst Parfaits

Preparation Time:
 1/2 hour + 1 hour
 refrigeration
Cooking Time:
 5 minutes
Makes 4

1 4-serving size
 package instant
 vanilla pudding
1 3-ounce package
 orange-flavored
 gelatin
1 cup boiling water
1 8 1/2-ounce can
 unpeeled apricot
 halves, drained and
 chopped
whipped cream, to
 serve
whole strawberries, to
 serve

1 Prepare instant pudding according to package directions. Spoon pudding evenly into 4 goblets or dessert dishes. Smooth top with a spoon or small metal spatula. Refrigerate until firm.
2 In a 2-cup glass measure combine gelatin and boiling water. Stir until all crystals have dissolved. Leave to cool to room temperature.
3 Divide the apricots evenly between goblets; pour gelatin evenly over apricots.

Refrigerate until set.
4 Just before serving, decorate with whipped cream and strawberries.

Note: Serve Sunburst Parfaits in small plastic wine goblets, available from supermarkets.

Apricot Fluff

Preparation Time:
 10 minutes
Cooking Time:
 None
Makes 4–6 servings

1/3 cup ricotta cheese
1/2 cup vanilla yogurt
1 tablespoon honey
1 1/2 cups apricot nectar
6 ice cubes
fresh fruit, to garnish
4–6 small paper
 umbrellas

1 Place ricotta cheese, yogurt, honey, nectar and ice cubes in a blender container. Cover and blend until smooth.
2 Pour the mixture into 4–6 clear plastic cups; garnish with fruit and an umbrella.

Note: Make Apricot Fluff just before serving because the mixture may separate if left to stand.

Apricot Fluff (left), Sunburst Parfaits (right).

1. For Layered Ice Cream Cups: Add caramel topping to ice cream; beat well.

2. Divide the mixture between 8 clear plastic cups.

3. Beat chocolate ice cream with electric beaters until smooth.

4. Add a few drops of red food coloring to the whipped cream mixture.

Layered Ice Cream Cups

Preparation Time:
15 minutes +
overnight freezing
Cooking Time:
None
Makes 8 small cups

Caramel layer
1 quart vanilla ice
cream
1 cup caramel ice
cream topping

Chocolate layer
1 quart chocolate ice
cream

Topping
1 cup heavy cream
1/4 cup strawberry
preserves
red food coloring,
optional

1 To make Caramel layer: Using electric beaters, beat ice cream until soft. Add caramel topping and beat until well combined. Divide evenly between 8 cups; smooth top. Freeze 5 hours or until firm.

2 To make Chocolate layer: Using electric beaters, beat chocolate ice cream until soft. Divide evenly between the cups. Spread chocolate layer evenly over caramel ice cream layer and smooth top. Return to freezer overnight.

3 To make Topping: Using electric beaters, beat heavy cream in medium bowl until soft peaks form. Add strawberry preserves, flavoring and a few drops of red food coloring, if desired. Beat until stiff peaks form. Just before serving, spoon the mixture into a large piping bag fitted with a star piping nozzle. Pipe swirls onto each ice cream cup or dollop top of each serving with whipped cream mixture. Serve immediately.

Note: For the caramel layer, a quick and easy option is to use caramel-swirl ice cream or a flavored ice cream such as toffee crunch or pralines and pecans. Beat desired flavor ice cream with electric beaters until soft, then continue as directed in the recipe. Any flavor ice cream, for both layers, can be used.

HINT
Take advantage of seasonal fruits to make a summer party fruit salad. Combine chopped fresh fruit in a large bowl, sprinkle with lemon juice and sugar to taste. Cover and refrigerate 2 hours. Serve in a watermelon hollowed out and carved into a boat or basket.

Pineapple Cream Crush

Preparation Time:
  5 minutes
Cooking Time:
  None
Makes about 4 cups

1 15¼-ounce can
  crushed pineapple
1 cup pineapple juice
3/4 cup sweetened
  coconut milk
pineapple slices

1 Combine crushed pineapple and 1 cup juice in a large pitcher or measuring cup.
2 Slowly pour in the coconut milk, whisking continually until well blended. Pour into tall glasses, garnish with pineapple slices and serve immediately.

Homemade Lemonade

Preparation Time:
  10 minutes + 2 hours standing
Cooking Time:
  5 minutes
Makes 2 quarts

1 cup sugar
1 cup water
3 tablespoons finely
  grated lemon peel
1 cup lemon juice
6 cups water, extra

1 Combine sugar and water in a small heavy-based pan. Stir over medium heat without boiling until sugar has completely dissolved. Brush sugar crystals from side of pan with a wet pastry brush. Bring to a boil; reduce heat slightly, and boil for 1 minute. Remove from heat; let cool.
2 Combine lemon peel, lemon juice and extra water in a large jug and add the cooled syrup. Let stand for 2 hours; strain and refrigerate. Serve over ice.

Witches' Brew

Preparation Time:
  5 minutes
Cooking Time:
  None
Makes 6 cups

2½ cups cola
6 small scoops vanilla
  ice cream
1 tablespoon
  strawberry syrup
12 gummy snakes, to
  decorate

1 Divide cola evenly between six glasses. Add a scoop of ice cream to each glass. Stir gently to foam (mixture will 'boil over' if stirred too hard).
2 Drizzle ½ teaspoon of syrup onto each drink. Hang 2 snakes over the side of each cup. Serve immediately.

Sunshine Punch

Preparation Time:
  5 minutes + 1 hour refrigeration
Cooking Time:
  None
Makes about 10 cups

3½ cups unsweetened
  pineapple juice
3½ cups apple juice
1 15½-ounce can
  crushed pineapple
3 cups lemonade or
  ginger ale, chilled

1 In a large serving bowl combine the pineapple and apple juices with the crushed pineapple; stir lightly to combine. Cover and refrigerate for 1 hour or until well chilled.
2 Just before serving, add the lemonade or ginger ale to pineapple mixture. Serve immediately.

Note: Substitute orange juice for apple juice, if desired.

Clockwise from top: Homemade Lemonade, Sunshine Punch, Pineapple Cream Crush and Witches' Brew.

Meteor Ice Cream Cones

Preparation Time:
  20 minutes
Cooking Time:
  5 minutes
Makes 8

4 ounces semisweet
  chocolate, chopped
2 tablespoons vegetable
  shortening
8 small ice cream cup
  cones
16 scoops ice cream
candy-coated chocolate
  pieces, to decorate

1 Place chocolate and shortening in a medium heatproof bowl. Place over pan of simmering water. Stir until they have melted and mixture is smooth. Cool slightly.
2 Place 2 scoops of very cold ice cream in each ice cream cone, packing it in firmly. Working one at a time, carefully dip the top of the ice cream into the warm chocolate mixture. Drain off excess chocolate. While the chocolate is still warm, press a few chocolate pieces on to decorate. Repeat with remaining ingredients. Serve immediately.

Tropical Slush

Preparation Time:
  10 minutes +
  overnight freezing
Cooking Time:
  None
Makes 8 cups

1 15½-ounce can
  tropical fruit salad
1 15½-ounce can
  crushed pineapple
3 cups fruit juice

1 Line an 8-inch square cake pan with foil, extending it over two sides. Pour all ingredients into prepared pan; stir, cover and freeze overnight.
2 Using foil, lift frozen mixture from the pan. Break into chunks. Place in food processor or blender (in two batches, if necessary) and process until it becomes slushy.
3 To serve, spoon into tall glasses. Serve immediately.

Frozen Banana Bites

Preparation Time:
  10 minutes + 2 hours
  freezing
Cooking Time:
  5 minutes
Makes 18

3 large bananas
9 wooden popsicle
  sticks
3 ounces semisweet
  chocolate, chopped
2 tablespoons vegetable
  shortening

1 Line a baking sheet with foil. Cut each banana into 6 pieces. Cut popsicle sticks in half. Carefully push a half-stick into each piece of banana.
2 Combine chocolate and shortening in a small heatproof bowl. Place over a pan of simmering water; stir until melted and mixture is smooth.
3 Working one at a time, dip each banana piece into hot chocolate mixture. Drain off any excess chocolate. Place on prepared baking sheet. Refrigerate until chocolate is set. Store in an airtight container in the freezer at least 2 hours before serving.

Note: Frozen Banana Bites should be eaten on the day they are made.

Clockwise from left: Meteor Ice Cream Cones, Tropical Slush and Frozen Banana Bites.

Choc-Orange Mousse

Preparation Time:
  20 minutes + 4–24
  hours refrigeration
Cooking Time:
  15 minutes
Serves 6

½ *cup sugar*
½ *cup orange juice*
4 *ounces semisweet*
  chocolate, chopped
2 *beaten eggs*
½ *cup heavy cream*
1 *teaspoon grated*
  orange peel

1 In a small saucepan combine sugar and orange juice. Cook and stir over medium heat until sugar dissolves. Add chocolate and cook over low heat until chocolate melts and mixture is smooth.
2 Gradually stir the chocolate mixture into beaten eggs. Return mixture to saucepan. Bring to a gentle boil. Cook and stir for 2 minutes more. Cool to lukewarm, stirring occasionally.
3 Beat the heavy cream and orange peel until soft peaks form. Add chocolate mixture and fold together until well combined.

4 Spoon chocolate mixture into six dessert dishes or bowls. Cover and chill for 4 to 24 hours before serving.

Smart-Alec Splits

Preparation Time:
  10 minutes + 30
  minutes refrigeration
  +1 hour freezing
Cooking Time:
  None
Makes 4

1 *pint vanilla ice cream*
¼ *cup strawberry*
  syrup
2 *bananas*
4 *tablespoons chocolate*
  syrup
candy-coated chocolate
  pieces, to decorate

1 Remove ice cream from freezer. Allow to soften in refrigerator for 30 minutes. Drizzle the strawberry syrup over ice cream and swirl through gently with a fork. Return to freezer for 1 hour or until frozen.
2 Cut bananas in half lengthwise. Place one banana half in each bowl and top with 2 small scoops ice cream and candy-coated chocolate syrup. Top with chocolate pieces. Serve immediately.

Smart-Alec Splits (top), Choc-Orange Mousse (bottom).

Index